Breathe

Breathe

The Simple Guide to Better Health for Quilters, Artists, and Creatives

By Kelly Sheets

Thanks to Jeff Sanders for the stellar cover design.

Connect with Jeff at ArtOfVitality.com.

Thank you to Valori Wells for sharing her *Morning Chatter* quilt for the cover from her May 2019 collection.

Find her at StitchinPost.com

Thanks to Linda Hanson for the author pics.

Check out her amazing artwork and photography at LearningToDrawWater.com

*"For breath is life, so if you breathe well
you will live long on earth."*

- Sanskrit proverb

"Improper breathing is a common cause of ill health."

- Dr. Andrew Weil

"Insufficient oxygen means insufficient biological energy. That can result in anything from mild fatigue to life-threatening disease. The link between insufficient oxygen and disease has now been firmly established."

- Dr. W. Spencer Way – Journal of the American Association of Physicians

Foreword by Jenny Doan

I was sitting in a cafe in Bali recently, taking in all the sights, sounds, and sensations of this wondrously beautiful place. I'd been in Indonesia for a week at that point, having just completed a retreat experience that was nothing short of life-changing. Sitting across from me at the table in that cafe was Kelly Sheets, one of the two women who led that transformational retreat, and who also happens to be the author of this book you're about to read.

I'd invited Kelly to lunch that day to try to find a way to express my gratitude for her work, and to share the spark of an idea I'd had earlier that week while immersed in the experience Kelly and her partner, artist and fabric designer Valori Wells, were creating.

The retreat Kelly and Valori hosted was designed specifically for people like you and me; creatives. They invited all types, including Quilters, Writers, Designers, Painters, Fiber Artists, Seamstresses, Storytellers, Branding Specialists, Stylists, Teachers, and more, with the intention of helping people like us find deep fulfillment in our creative expression and in our lives in general. Valori brought the cutting edge and culturally significant artistic activities and Kelly brought the practices to increase self-awareness and unleash creativity in all areas of life.

And unleash we did.

At lunch that day in that Balinese cafe, I told Kelly what I was thinking. I shared with her how much I love my community. The quilters who follow me are a special group of humans unlike any other I've ever known. Their love and support over the years has made my life and business more fulfilling and vibrant than I'd ever imagined possible. And so I love to find opportunities to give back some joy and fulfillment to them whenever I can.

Each December, I share a high-value resource with my community. I carefully curate something that I think will help them in the coming year. And since I know how big the hearts of my people are - and how they often give, give, give to others before filling their own cup - I try to find a resource that will help them put themselves first in the new year to come.

For this year, Kelly is my gift to my community. The work she introduced me to in Bali made such an enormous impact on my ability to fill my own cup, feel fulfilled, and dive deeper into my own creativity, that I couldn't wait to introduce her and her transformational work to my community.

Creatives like us often spend hours sitting or standing to do the thing we love most. As most of us know, prolonged sitting and standing can contribute to decreased health in many ways. After our conversation over lunch in Bali, we decided, that along with an instructional video made especially for my community on YouTube, Kelly would create a simple guide to specifically help Quilters, Artists, and Creatives like us to increase our awareness of our breath and to offer simple practices to help us increase our health.

This book is an adaptation of Kelly's first published work, recrafted especially for the quilting community. Breathing is one of the many things Kelly teaches her clients. It's often her go-to fundamental suggestion for people because it helps cultivate change instantly.

Forward

Breathing in an intentional way, as Kelly suggests in this book, can change the quality of your life. Kelly shared with me that in her work with older adults, by implementing breathing practices alone, she saw many changes occur for participants – including altered perspectives, increased range of motion, increased sense of well-being, improved self-awareness, and deeper relationships with their bodies.

The combination of the breathing practices and stretches in this book will help you experience how important healthy breathing is to your quality of life. My hope is that you will give your breath the attention it deserves, keeping yourself healthy and vibrant, so you can begin to unleash all the potential within your own self and creativity like I, myself, have done with Kelly's help.

Here's to your unleashed creativity and best health!

Jenny Doan

Missouri Star Quilt Co

Table of Contents

Introduction

Introduction

Being able to live fully and feel engaged in our lives requires that our physical bodies be well. Often when we are in creative mode, we are sitting or standing for long periods of time, which definitely can have ill effects on all the systems in our bodies.

Many people tend to resist starting a fitness program or feel unmotivated to do something new even though they know they "should." This guide can help you feel changes quickly and move toward being a healthier you.

Breathing is something humans do every minute of every day, mostly without thinking. Most people have never been taught how the quality of their breathing patterns affects their life.

When you breathe fully, you improve your energy levels and the health of your body. The patterns and rhythms of your breath, or the way you breathe, directly affect your emotional, mental, physical, and spiritual states.

This book will give you an understanding of how to breathe and to start a breathing practice, even if you have never paid attention to your breath before. You will also gain a better understanding of how it affects your overall health. These practices offer mental, physical, and emotional wellness.

Improving your breathing capacity can be particularly helpful as you age, not just physically, but mentally and emotionally as well, and I will address that. That said, the information contained in this book pertains to everyone and learning this at a young age can set you up for a lifetime of healthy breathing, a healthy body, and clarity of mind.

Meditation in this book simply refers to a focused practice of observing how you breathe and what you feel in your body while breathing. Throughout the book I will use the terms meditation and breathing practice interchangeably.

The information and tools I share in this book are an accumulation of my personal practice and exploration while teaching yoga. It is simply an introduction to your breath.

How To Use This Book

This book is primarily written concepts, but I have included short practices throughout the book which prompt you to stop and pay attention to your body.

There are also links to my website where you can listen to recorded sessions. You can use the recordings during your meditations or listen to them until you become comfortable enough to meditate quietly on your own.

The links to the recorded sessions are on pg. 55. The meditations are also written out so you can read them. The only way to really understand how you are breathing and how it affects your life is to take the time to pay attention, feel, explore, and experiment.

There are a few sections you should read before getting started to be certain you understand the power of your breath and precautions to take.

Please do not skip these two sections:

Preparing for a Breathing Practice - pg. 6

Guiding Your Breath vs. Pushing - pg. 31

Preparing for a Breathing Practice

While learning to breathe more efficiently, you should be aware that your breath is powerful and affects all the systems of your body. You should observe yourself and practice listening to the signs and symptoms your body is constantly giving you.

A few signs that you may be controlling your breath too much and need to allow your breath to return to normal:

- You were able to breathe in and out of your nose at the start of the meditation but now you need to open your mouth to catch your breath or to feel at ease.
- You begin to feel light-headed or start to feel nauseous.
- You abruptly begin to feel irritated or agitated.

These are signs that you need to breathe easier. These symptoms can arise if you are holding or controlling your breath or using excessive effort to breathe deeply.

Breathing & Meditation

What Is Meditation?

Meditation is not a way of making your mind quiet. It's a way of entering into the quiet that's already there – buried under the 50,000 thoughts the average person thinks every day.

~ Deepak Chopra

There are many different types of meditation and they are used for different purposes such as relaxation, contemplation, physical transformation, dealing with emotional or mental issues, etc. Meditation is training the mind to gain a desired result. It is not religious, but it is a tool that many religions use.

You can meditate on something such as an image or the movement of your breath or the sound of a chant. People also meditate on a philosophical concept, breaking it down and examining it, trying to understand it deeply, sitting quietly without distraction. You can do the same examination with your breath or emotions you feel, as well as examining what you feel in your physical body. You pay focused attention to something during meditation. There are many resources on the Internet if you are interested in learning more about the various types of meditation.

When I refer to meditation in this book and in the work I do, I specifically mean paying attention to the breath and what you feel in your body. For me, meditation is a tool I use to become more aware of my current situation, more aware of the health of my breath and my thoughts, and what sensations I feel in my body. Meditation is a time when I quietly pay attention to what is happening in my life. I also use it as a way to understand what's going on physically in my body.

When I lead people in meditation, I ask them to keep their attention on what is happening in that moment. They are breathing no matter what else is going on. So, I ask them to focus on how their breathing patterns are changing. Sometimes I lead them through stretches while they pay attention to their breath. Moving in time with their breath, they can constantly observing how it is changing. They watch their breath become shorter and longer, shallower or deeper, and faster or slower. They also pay attention to how their body feels, how their mind changes when their breathing patterns change, and the way their breath changes as different emotions arise.

The more aware you are of how your emotions change and your body feels as your breath changes, the more connected you will be to your body. You will feel more in control of your body's experience. You can begin to experiment and feel new things simply by changing how you breathe and ultimately shifting the sensations in your body.

For example, as you slouch forward and restrict your breathing capacity, you may become anxious. This is the body's response to shallow or restricted breathing. Once you learn and experience that sitting up straight and breathing fully can relieve this anxiety, you change your experience, empowering you to feel more in control. You will pay more attention to sitting up straight, creating more space for your lungs to expand, and breathing more fully.

Meditation is called a "practice" because it takes practice to pay attention, continue to breathe fully and stay focused on what is happening in the moment. It takes practice to move past the resistance you have to sit still, to listen, to focus, and to feel what is happening in your body without moving or getting distracted. It takes practice to watch your thoughts and not get swept away to the past or future – to stay in the here and now, breathing. It is a practice of discipline. When learning something new, you must practice and for most people, paying attention to their breath is a new experience.

Benefits of Healthy Breathing

Remember that old song "The hip bone is connected to the thigh bone?" Well it's true, everything is connected. The systems of your body are not separate. The health of your breath affects every system of the body in some way. When you breathe fully and completely, there are many benefits – physical, emotional, and mental. Some benefits of healthy breathing are:

Physical:

- Increases mental and physical alertness.
- Helps to reduce pain by decreasing the tension that contributes to pain.
- Opens up the chest area to make breathing easier and fuller.
- Helps eliminate waste matter through exhaling.
- Improves blood circulation, and other fluid circulation in the body.
- Increases supply of oxygen and nutrients to cells throughout the body.
- Calms or stimulates the nervous system – depending on the needs of the individual.
- Massages the internal organs, aiding in their function.
- Helps push the movement of lymph throughout the body, which helps to eliminate waste, reduce swelling, and strengthen the immune system.
- Relaxes you and helps you become more connected with your deepest sense of self.

- Reduces and releases muscular tension that eventually may cause structural problems and spasms.

- Helps increase flexibility and strength of joints and connective tissue for continued ease of breath; when you breathe easier you move easier.

Mental/Emotional:

The way you breathe affects the patterns of your thoughts. If you are breathing shallowly and rapidly your mind will follow. Shallow breathing triggers your sympathetic response system (your fight or flight system). For example, imagine someone approaching you from behind at night. You jump, lift your shoulders up, and take a quick shallow inhale. This is fear, and it triggers a fear response. The body triggers the fight or flight system when you are breathing shallowly, because it thinks you are in a stressful situation or might need to react quickly. In addition, the mind starts racing looking for threats and possible solutions.

When you breathe deeply and fully, your mind calms, and your thoughts are clearer. When you breathe fully and engage your diaphragm, the body triggers its parasympathetic system, which then releases calming chemicals into your body. A common example would be when you feel angry and someone suggests that you "count to ten." The idea is to breathe deeply and slowly while counting to ten, giving the body time to trigger the chemical system in the body that will calm the body and angry thoughts. You can feel the calming effects as you slow down and deepen your breath.

Also, the brain and body are affected by the levels of oxygen entering the body. If you are not breathing deeply and fully, you may not get sufficient oxygen into the body nor efficiently expel carbon dioxide. A lack of oxygen can certainly affect the ability of the brain to function optimally. For example, when you don't get enough oxygen your moods may change, your critical thinking may decrease, your judgment can become impaired, and your energy levels may decrease. And these results change the way you feel and act in your life.

If you are more aware of the fullness of your breath, you can be more in control of your state of mind, which in turn, will affect the body. Anxiety and fear responses can increase with age. This could be connected with fears of ill health or end of life thoughts, but it can also be related to a decrease in breathing capacity.

The benefit of being aware, of what is happening in your body and how fully you are breathing, is that you have more control. By this I mean, when you feel something happening in your body you can pay attention to your breath, change its rhythm, and then watch how it affects your body.

Creatively:

When creativity is flowing, it is a whole person experience. It is a mental, emotional, physical, energetic, and environmental experience.

What limits creative flow is tension. It is that simple. Tension reduces flow. So, reducing tension in all areas of our mind, body, energy, environment, and emotions increases the flow and gives us access to more possibilities and new ideas. Feeling these different parts of yourself takes practices and sensory awareness. A breathing practice is an excellent way to increase creative flow.

Basic Anatomy of Healthy Breathing

The lungs are encased in the rib cage. The ribs are the protective mechanism for these vital organs. You have two lungs and their job is to absorb oxygen and expel carbon dioxide. Muscles and connective tissue hold the ribs together. At the base of the rib cage sits a big, strong muscle called the diaphragm.

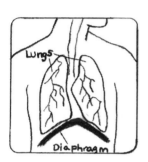

The diaphragm is what separates the lungs from the internal abdominal organs. It contracts down into the abdominal area on the inhale, massaging the internal organs while allowing a full oxygenated breath. On an exhale, it relaxes up to expel the air, waste, and carbon dioxide from the lungs. Effectively expelling carbon dioxide is as important to the health of your body as inhaling enough oxygen.

In healthy breathing, you inhale deeply and expand your lungs in all directions. The lungs and rib cage expand to the sides and front and back. The connective tissue between your ribs lengthens to allow expansion. The lungs also expand up and down. This results in a full, complete breath.

Try this short exercise to understand what it looks like, and feels like, to take a deep breath:

Close this book. Lay on your back. Relax and place the book on your belly button. As you breathe easily, your book will begin to rise and fall as your belly rises and falls. This is a result of your diaphragm contracting and expanding, pushing gently on your internal organs, in turn pushing your stomach gently out, lifting the book. Then when you exhale, your stomach and book move back toward the floor as your diaphragm moves back toward your lungs. As your breath deepens, the book will rise higher.

The flexibility of the tissues, and the health and integrity of all the muscles surrounding your rib cage will affect the amount of air you can take in. If the muscles and connective tissue around the ribs become stiff or inflexible your body will compensate by using the muscles up in your shoulder and neck area to help you inhale.

As you go through your day, observe the people you interact with. Watch as they breathe. Does their stomach move? Do their shoulders go up and down as they inhale and exhale? If their shoulders are rising, you may see the muscles in their neck tighten with the effort of inhaling.

The internal health of the lungs is important too. They need to remain soft and flexible inside. The air you breathe has waste in it and this can settle in the base of your lungs. Breathing deeply stimulates the soft internal tissues, moving around any toxins that may have settled. The toxins will be picked up and moved out on an exhale. If the internal area is hardened or tough, this job will not be performed as well and waste may begin to accumulate in the base of the lungs.

How Tension Affects Your Health

What is happening in the body as it ages? One thing for sure is that as you move less the tension in your body increases. Imagine young children on the playground, they are pliable, flexible, flipping all around; their bodies are fluid and can respond quickly. As people go through the middle years of their lives, they generally sit more and slow down. Once they reach their senior years, are often spending more time sitting than anything else. When people move less their muscles become less pliable, less fluid and tighten up.

When You Move You:

- Pump waste out of each system of the body.
- Move fluids to the joints to keep them moist and pliable.
- Bring nutrients to the spine to keep it flexible and moving.
- Intake more oxygen which moves through the body and into the brain, maintaining mental clarity.
- Keep muscles loose, allowing nerve signals to pass easily to the whole body.
- Increase the health of the heart and lungs.
- Increase feelings of well-being.

If you decrease the amount you move each day, the whole body is affected in a negative manner. The healthiest people I have known walk and move every day as much as they can. Consider having a daily walking routine. Walking is an excellent activity to stay healthy and it directly affects your lungs and breathing capacity. And as a bonus walking often seems to stimulate creative mojo!

Visualize: Your lungs are encased in your rib cage. When your body is healthy your lungs expand up and down and to the sides, front and back when you inhale. When your lungs expand so does your rib cage. (I like to imagine my lungs expanding in all directions like a balloon when I blow it up). When you exhale, your lungs expel waste and air and your rib cage relaxes.

At the very bottom of the lungs is the big muscle, the diaphragm (diagram on page 14) which moves down on the inhale and back up on the exhale. Now imagine if the tissues between your ribs got stiff or the diaphragm stopped moving up and down. The muscles at the top of your rib cage would have to start to work harder to expand your lungs upwards in an attempt to get a full inhale. The shoulders and neck would start to work harder to help you breathe. But if tension increased in your shoulders, back and upper chest from doing extra work or carrying many years of stress, this would limit your capacity to breathe even further. Your body will continue to make an effort to inhale all the air it needs, but if there is a lot of tension, a full breath may not be possible.

Imagine a man who has started to slouch forward in his chair while watching a few hours of TV. As a result of slouching, he has less space to expand his lungs so he is now taking in less oxygen and clean air and expelling less waste out of his lungs. Can you visualize how that will affect his health? He may have increased anxiety, increased risk of respiratory issues, decreased clarity in thoughts and memories, etc. Though it can be a result of disease, much of this increased tension around the lungs is simply a result of decreased movement and use.

You can release tension in your body by being aware of it, consciously relaxing, moving regularly, and stretching. Other tension is so chronic that to release it requires specific movement, deep relaxation, and massage.

If it feels like you just cannot take a deep, full breath you can gently reach along the underside of your ribs with your fingertips and massage the area. The diaphragm is a muscle and can be massaged like any other.

Continuing to move and breathe fully is how you keep the tissues in and around the lungs healthy. "Move it or lose it" is not just a saying – it is a reality. You can positively affect your life by creating a breathing practice and in turn create new habits.

The Logistics of Practicing

Sitting in a Healthy Way

To begin a breathing practice, it is helpful to get into a comfortable position that you can maintain throughout the time you are sitting. If you start meditating and then begin to feel uncomfortable, you will begin to move your attention away from your breath. You may have trouble focusing and begin to fidget. This is especially true if you do not exercise daily or have extra energy to burn.

A moving meditation is another option if you tend to be fidgety. In fact, I recommend exploring a moving meditation such as a walking meditation for quilters, creatives, and artists who tend to sit or stand for long periods of time while in creative mode. This will give you the benefits of moving while also exploring your breath.

Meditation can be practiced while sitting, standing, lying down, walking, doing yoga poses, running, etc. For now, I will focus on sitting in a chair since this is the simplest to access. How you sit will directly affect how you breathe, how comfortable you will be and most likely how long your meditation will last.

The best position for the body is to sit up straight with the head directly above the spine.

Try this as you are reading right now: Place your feet on the floor hip-width apart. Scoot back in your chair so your hips are gently touching the back of the chair.

23

If your back is not touching the chair, place a pillow behind your pelvis, a small firm one will do. The intention of the pillow is to support your hips and keep you sitting up tall. Your back should be upright, and your pelvis will tip forward a bit. Imagine the letter L. Your hips should bend at a 90-degree angle and the chair and pillow are used to support that position.

Allow your spine to be tall and long. Gently lift your chest and roll your shoulders back and then down. Now pull your chin back gently so your head is over your spine and look straight ahead. Feel the weight of your head over the top of your spine. From here, move your chin slowly forward and back. As you move it forward, it will feel heavier and you'll feel a strain on your neck. When you pull your head back, feel it line up on top of your spine and you will have less stress on the back of your neck. Exaggerate the movement so you can feel the weight of your head and the muscles used to hold it up.

One of the things you can observe as people age is that many walk around with their heads jutting out forward, ahead of them. This creates extra strain on their neck and also changes their overall posture in a non-beneficial way. It is often caused by sitting and rounding their shoulders forward.

Sitting for extended periods of time creates a tightness and shortening of the muscles and connective tissue in the front of your body including your hips, stomach, and chest areas - all which decrease your ability to breath fully. It also contributes to many other physical issues over time. Getting up and walking around is really helps to keep the front body pliable and moving - as well as activating your metabolism.

Anytime you are sitting is a good time to practice healthy posture, your head directly over your spine gently pulling the chin back toward the throat so you feel your head centered over your neck. Another visual is to line your ears up over your shoulders.

> **What do you feel? Sit back right now and feel how it feels to sit up straight and focus on your breath. Then slouch and focus on your breath again. Do this a few times until you can feel how much easier it is to breathe when you sit up straight**

You can see how the very first part of breathing well is good posture. Having good posture alone can completely change how you breathe.

Getting seated comfortably and with good posture also makes a breathing practice easier because if you become uncomfortable while sitting, your mind will wander to the discomfort in your body, rather than remain focused on your breath.

Continue to practice sitting up straight throughout the day so creating good postural habits. The muscles required to sit up straight may be weak and if this is the case, you will need to build up strength gradually by practicing.

Note: Breathing fully is your primary intention, so, if the suggestions for sitting create too much discomfort, simply sit however you can be most still and breathe most easily for your meditation time. Then, continue to practice sitting up tall and improving your posture at other times in the day.

Identifying Sensations and Why They Matter

Let's start by defining a sensation? A sensation is a physical feeling or perception in the body. There are names for many sensations such as tingling, warmth, coolness, numbness, vibration, pain, etc. Your practice during meditation can be to simply become aware of them. You do not need to name the sensations just notice what you are feeling. You should spend some time during every meditation scanning your body and becoming aware of what sensations are occurring.

Why do the sensations matter? Sensations arise in the body as indicators. They are signs and symptoms of things occurring within us, healthy and unhealthy. Most people don't know what they are feeling and are unaware of the subtle sensations in their bodies. But when you are aware of them you can make changes if they are symptoms of disease or continue on if they are symptoms of health.

For example, I have an old back injury. When I am not taking good care to stretch my hips, I start to get a pinching feeling in the arch of my foot. If I ignore that pinching, over a week's time, I can have cramping in my low back, a pinching in the left side of my stomach next to my belly button and then pain in my sciatic nerve. When I was younger, I did not have a clue that all those sensations were symptoms of upcoming major pain in my leg. In fact, I mostly didn't even take notice of them. Now, every day, I feel for sensations, in my legs and hips, watch for the symptoms and learned to stretch more deeply when the arch of my foot starts to feel "pinchy." This way I can avoid the debilitating pain in my back.

On an emotional level, if you become more aware of the sensations in your body, you can feel what triggers your emotions and be prepared to respond to them. Many people think emotional states like anxiety, stress, overwhelm, and frustration are states that we just have to deal with and everyone has them. But that is not true. Through my work with clients and myself, I know that when we get intimate with our sensations, we can eliminate these states. For example, through a recent survey we confirmed that 100% of our clients significantly reduced or completely eliminated anxiety.

For example, just before I react with anger, I feel my throat, jaw and chest tighten and energy starts swirling in my head. When I feel these sensations, I stop and become aware that I am about to react before I say something foolish. I take a full breath to release tension and engage my diaphragm. When the tension releases, the sensations change. Then I can choose to respond to the situation rather than react.

Examples of a few sensations you may feel in your body:

Warmth	Tingling	Pinching	Dullness
Pulling	Shivering	Numbness	Tightness
Swirling	Pulsing	Aching	Vibrating

For a full list of over 100 different sensations go to: **www.KellySheets.com/breathe**

The human body is an amazing, complex system. There are so many sensations that most people are not aware of nor feel. Most of my clients cannot identify what they are feeling at first. Reading the full list may give you a broader sense of what to be aware of. Sitting quietly in meditation is a good way to practice this awareness.

One of the intentions of a regular breathing practice is increasing your awareness of what is going on inside your body. You can learn to put aside the million thoughts passing through your head and focus on your body and what signals it is sending you.

A side note about pain, emotional and physical. Use your breathing practice to experiment with how your breath affects these experiences. Your experience of sensations can be changed often by broadening or narrowing your range of attention.

For example, if you feel pain in your neck, also become aware of your whole body. Everything is connected, so check if softening your belly, or jaw or chest, changes the feelings of pain. I find that tension in other areas of the body, which may seem unrelated to the pain, can heighten the intensity of all sensations.

You may also go right into the center of the pain and feel the sensations that are there beyond the general label of pain. As you breathe and give it attention you may observe the sensations change. The experience of pain can change, breath by breath, moment to moment.

Practicing is important so that when you have feelings that you perceive as "bad" or overwhelming, you can stop resisting them and begin to understand how to resolve them.

Eventually your breathing practice becomes second nature. You can be doing something and simultaneously feeling sensations so that you are fluidly aware of what you are doing and feeling moment to moment. This gives you access to a higher state of health because you can respond and make choices that align with your intentions to be healthy.

Why Humans Avoid Sitting Quietly

When you begin to sit and listen to your breath you will have many reactions emotionally and physically. Normally, internally and externally, people keep themselves very busy and don't pay attention to what is going on inside. One of their greatest fears is finding out what is happening in their own mind. People tend to go through decades of their lives without ever spending much quiet time alone. They turn on the television, listen to music, pick up a book, go to the gym, take care of their children, work, and create distractions in their lives so that even when they have free time, it is not free.

And then when the outside is quiet, the mind is analyzing, pontificating, labeling, judging, and story creating. Geez, sounds exhausting ... and it literally is. We exhaust our energetic resources, which could be used for meaningful interactions and projects, on this internal and external busyness.

Think of yourself. How often do you sit quietly without thinking of what you need to do, or what is coming next, or what has already happened? It is a practice in discipline to sit through that time and explore what comes up for you.

Question: What fears or emotions arise in you when you sit quietly. If you start to fidget and think a lot, what are the predominant thoughts?

Fear can cause a physical reaction in the body. When I did my first long, quiet meditation in 2009, a full week of silence, I became physically sick. I sat the first evening for two quiet hours and then suddenly I had to run to the bathroom because

I was sick. I felt the terror of quiet overwhelm me and more specifically the fear of what insights I might learn. Fortunately, after I got sick, I was able to relax and explore the quiet time. And I did have major insights that changed my life for the better. Yes, those realizations were scary to think about but when I acted on them, they helped me create a much more fulfilling, loving, and kind life.

It is common to have a fear of being quiet. Most people have no idea what will fill that quiet space.

Of course, unless some tragic medical issue occurs during the meditation, you will be fine. It is the fear of the unknown that causes people to avoid meditating and quietly observing their breath.

Having a comfortable space to sit quietly or choosing to walk quietly in nature may help you feel emotionally safe enough to explore what you feel.

Guiding Your Breath vs. Pushing

Imagine yourself jumping into a pool and holding your breath. If you are under the water long enough your lungs begin to burn and panic arises that you will never breathe again. Let's call that "pushing," or forcing you to use your breath a certain way. You are pushing yourself to hold your breath in order to survive.

Now, imagine holding your nose and going under the water in the shallow end. You are completely safe, your feet are on the ground and you will come up when you are ready. You no longer feel stress because you know you are in control, you can relax your body and you will come up for air when you are ready. You realize that you can hold your breath even longer because you relax and feel in control. Let's call this "guiding."

During your breathing practice, you should always be "guiding" and never "pushing." You should feel that you can remain relaxed with your breath and feel no pressure to hold it longer or control it in any certain way. You may have tension in your breath and body from years of shallow breathing or an increasingly sedentary life, so start gently.

One of the reasons for meditation is to become aware of and decrease tension in your breathing pattern. Pushing is equal to increasing tension. When you push another person, they resist. When you push your breath, your body resists by getting tight or increasing tension. There are appropriate practices that are available for controlling the breath, but these tools should only be learned from a qualified professional.

Imagine the tension around your chest area and then imagine it relaxing as you breathe during meditation. As the tension around your ribs and chest releases, your lungs can expand more fully with less effort. Keep this visual in your mind. You will need to continually remind yourself to soften and release tension along the way. This should be something you focus on during every breathing practice. The intention is to decrease tension and increase your capacity to breathe fully.

Part of paying attention is exploration. You can explore relaxing or tensing specific muscles around the chest and abdominal areas and noticing how it affects your ability to breathe. Be curious. See if you can identify sensations and notice things you have never noticed before.

Stretches to Get the Flow Going

One of the simplest ways to breathe better is by doing stretches to lengthen the muscles around the rib cage and the muscles that support breathing. Just like changing your posture, stretching can have an immediate effect on your breathing capacity. I suggest stretching every morning when you get up, even if it is just for a few minutes, as well before you start your breathing practice.

Imagine a cat or dog just after they wake up from a nap. They almost immediately stretch their whole body including the sides of the rib cage. It is a natural, often automatic response to keep the areas around the rib cage and lungs pliable. In order to maintain pliability as you age and move less, you should make it a conscious practice to actively stretch. A few chest opening stretches can help you breathe more fully.

How Stretching Affects Health:

To explain the stiffness you feel in your body each morning, visualize all your connective tissues shrinking as you sleep ... like shrink wrap. The connective tissue in the body is in a constant movement towards shrinking. This shrinking is beneficial because it keeps you together in one piece as a human. But if not stretched, the connective tissue can squeeze the body so it is no longer fluid and flexible, which will impede the body's healthy function.

The diaphragm (page 14) is like any other muscle in the body. It gets weak if you don't use it and if you hold it tight for long enough and it will become chronically tight. Often the diaphragm gets stiff because people in many cultures, particularly women, are taught to "hold your belly in." Holding the belly in can limit the movement of the diaphragm. In seeking a flat stomach, you can create a chronic pattern that inhibits healthy breathing.

Remember that everything is connected. If this area locks up, you can't breathe deeply, the fight or flight response is constantly being triggered, keeping the body in a constant state of low-grade stress. Ultimately, the hormonal system becomes fatigued by continually sending out chemicals trying to "help you," which can result in the overall feeling of low-grade fatigue.

Stretching the chest and diaphragm daily keeps them pliable, increasing your ability to take a full, easy breath.

What Stretching Feels Like:

When stretching these areas you may actually feel an instant increase in energy. The release of tension from stretching also releases built up energy, making that energy available for your use.

You may feel an increase in anxiety as you stretch if your diaphragm is locked up and tight. If you feel like you can't take a deep breath, stretch more gently and allow yourself to breathe easy.

When stretching you should not be "pushing" the body for the same reasons you don't want to "push" the breath. Imagine your muscles have a personality; if you push them to stretch, they will resist. They need to feel safe and relaxed to stretch deeper. Muscles relax on the exhale so if you want to stretch more deeply, do it on an exhale. Inhale, get into position and on the exhale, gently stretch.

More is not better! Paying attention to what you feel and relaxing (or softening) is better. When pushed to stretch more, the body increases its stress and resistance. Start slowly and feel what is happening in your body. This is all an exploration.

A quick note on the word "relax." If you have been carrying tension around in your body for years, you may not really understand what it feels like to be relaxed or how to get your body to relax. I like to substitute "soften" and sometimes "melt" to give a visual of what relaxing might feel like. You may find some other word that will work equally well.

10 Seated Stretches:

These stretches focus on the areas that will increase movement in the rib cage, neck, and shoulders.

- **Shrugging Shoulders:** Lift shoulders up towards ears and then shrug down. Do this 10 times.

- **Shoulder Circles:** Move shoulders in big circles forward 10 times and then backward 10 times. Repeat – but this time make big square shapes instead of circles.

- **Chest Opener:** Reach arms behind back and clasp fingers together pulling elbows closer together. At the same time pushing breastbone forward and lift chest. If you can't reach hands, effort as if you are reaching to touch hands in the back and still lift your chest. Or hold a belt between your hands behind your back and move your hands closer along the belt as your chest stretches.

- **Side Stretches:** Raising arms over-head, clasp hands togeth er and reach up, up, up and slightly to the right. Repeat to left side. If you cannot get your arms up over your head, raise them up as much as you can with the intention of stretching the sides of your ribs

- **Side Benders**: Sit up tall. Let arms hang at sides. One side at a time, reach down as if picking something off of the floor. Then come back to center and reach down to the opposite side. Do not lean forward, this movement should be directly to the side (side bend). You will not be able to reach the floor but that is the direction you are reaching. It will stretch the sides of the ribcage.

- **Head Turning:** Side to Side: Start with head looking forward. Lengthen your neck by gently lifting the top of your head towards the ceiling. Relax shoulders down away from ears. Keep shoulders facing forward and look over right shoulder as far as possible – slowly. Hold for count of 5. Go back to neutral and repeat on the left side.

- **Ear to Shoulder**: Head in neutral position, looking forward. Relax shoulders down away from ears. Allow right ear to fall to right shoulder. Keep left shoulder down where it started. Hold 5 counts. Lift head back up to neutral. Do opposite on the left side.

- **Spine Rounding:** Sitting up tall. Begin pushing chest forward while shoulders pull back. Reverse and push shoulders forward while breastbone pulls back. This will create an arching and rounding of the upper back. Round and arch 10 times.

- **Pelvis Rocking**: Sit up straight. Focus on belly button and begin moving it forward and back. This will begin rocking the hips/pelvis forward and back. Do this 10 times.

- **Jaw Rotations**: Open mouth wide. Move upper and lower jaw side to side 5 times. Open and close mouth as wide as possible 5 times.

Creating a Space to Sit

An environment that is welcoming, warm, and friendly creates a safe space for your breathing practice. When you begin paying attention to your breath, being in a safe place may feel important or helpful to creating a consistent curious practice. You may feel changes in your body or emotions and feel like this is a completely new experience. You may not feel much - just be open to whatever occurs. The space you choose may affect your ability to get settled, sit still, and focus.

Details such as the temperature of the room, what the room smells like, or the lighting are all aspects of a creating an environment. In the beginning, when the mind may not be as cooperative, the external factors in the room may affect your ability to focus.

Choose A Space:

Choosing a room or space for your breathing practice is important when you are just beginning. If a quiet room is available, like a guest room or home office, that is perfect. The room should have a door you can close for privacy.

If you are going to use a space in your home where many people live you may want to consider making yourself a sign for the door. Your sign can simply let people know that when they see the door closed and the sign hung, not to disturb you because you are meditating.

> **Please, Do Not Disturb,**
> **I am Meditating. Thanks!**

Time of the Day:

It's good to meditate any time of the day. The more the merrier! Choose times of the day that are optimal and most beneficial for you. A breathing practice may make you feel deeply relaxed or it may energize you. If you start the day with a meditation, you will be more aware throughout the day. When you end the day with a meditation, you will be relaxed and it may help you sleep better. You may find that breathing creates an alert state and would keep you awake. As you explore you will learn what works for you.

Generally, it is recommended to meditate before eating or a couple hours after a meal. Immediately after eating, you may feel lethargic and this can make you feel sleepy during meditation, rather than alert and focused.

How Long Should You Meditate?

This depends on your preference. I would start out with ten minutes initially. I suggest stretching for ten minutes, sitting for a ten-minute meditation followed by sitting quietly for five minutes to review how you felt during the meditation. If you have not meditated quietly before, ten minutes can be a good starting length for the breathing portion. You can increase the length as you get comfortable. Setting a timer can help you keep your focus on the moment.

Honestly, for some people ten minutes can feel like an eternity when starting to pay attention! Just be curious with it. You are the boss and the whole mission is to get curious and feel something new.

How Often Should You Meditate?

Again, this depends on your preference, your time availability, and your interest. You might try twice a day for ten to twenty minutes. There is no amount of time or repetition that is required to benefit from paying attention to your breath. Every time you sit quietly and pay attention, you benefit by becoming more aware of your breath and getting to know yourself better. I find that the more I do it, the more curious I am and the subtler things I notice. And it gets more fun.

Practicing daily will create a rhythm to your breathing practice and a quicker understanding of your breath and your body. But I think it is better to start simple, increasing the duration and repetition as you get more comfortable and have a desire to increase.

Lighting:

Create a space where the lighting is not too bright so that your eyes can relax. Natural light is best. If the lighting is too bright you may not be able to pay attention as easily to your breath or if they are too dim you may become sleepy. As your practice and your focus on your breath improves, these details will not matter so much.

Music:

Whether or not you use background music depends on your preference. Music creates a certain feeling in the environment. It affects you emotionally, mentally, and physically. I don't use music because I want to focus internally not on the external world, which I otherwise do all day long.

When I was teaching yoga, if my intention was to help the participants relax, I may play some light music with no lyrics in the background. You may find that it actually helps you to focus inwards. Listen to many types of music and feel how you are affected by it. In the beginning, I suggest focusing on the silence and leaving out the added distraction of the music. After a few weeks try it out and see what works for you.

Aromas:

Your sense of smell is connected to your memories and emotions. Everyone has had the experience of a specific scent immediately triggering a memory from years ago. It can feel as if the memory is happening again. An article in the New York Times stated: "Importantly, the olfactory cortex is embedded within the brain's limbic system and amygdala, where emotions are born and emotional memories stored. That's why smells, feelings and memories become so easily and intimately entangled."

During my personal meditation, I burn incense. This has a strong smell that triggers my mind that it's time to pay attention to my breath and focus inward. If you use the same scent during every meditation, it will become a habitual trigger that it is time to pay attention to your breath.

I recommend a mild aromatherapy scent with pure essential oils. You can purchase aromatherapy essential oils with an electric warmer. Synthetic chemical scents, while cheaper, can be irritating and dissipate less easily into the air than essential oils. Lavender is the most commonly used calming essential oil. It is relaxing and won't harm your skin should you touch it. You can explore different essential oil scents and how they affect your ability to focus.

How to Handle Distractions

When you first begin to meditate it may seem like every little noise distracts you from focusing on your breath. This will get better as you practice.

What should you do if there are noises outside of the room that become distracting? If the space is noisy or you expect there to be disruptions while meditating, you can put headphones on or use earplugs. The better you get at focusing, the easier it will be to ignore or not give value to the distractions.

Another distraction that will occur is that your mind will begin thinking "off-topic." When your mind begins to wander away to other subjects, take notice and gently bring your attention back to your breath. The mind is a busy place and it likes to share its opinions and ideas, remind you of all the things you forgot to do before sitting down to meditate and most likely tell you this is a waste of time. If we spoke out loud all the thoughts going through in our minds, we would drive each other crazy.

Be kind to yourself if you are having trouble focusing. Some days are better than others as far as a calm mind goes. The focus here is to attend to your breath and sensations in your body not to make the thoughts stop. Trying to get them to stop can be a distraction in itself.

Another distraction may occur if you choose to meditate with your eyes open. In certain schools of meditation the eyes always remain open and slightly cast down. Try it. It may be distracting as you get used to tuning out the sensory stimuli around you. You may want to start by closing your eyes and then as you get better at focusing, open your eyes and feel the difference.

Knowing your intention is very important. When you have a clear intention, it can help to dissipate the fear of sitting still and help decrease the amount that outside distractions actually disrupt your attention. My suggestion is to make "exploration of the breath and awareness of sensations" be the primary intention and the secondary intention to "be curious and kind to self."

If exploration is the intention, you can be open to anything that happens during the quiet time because you are simply exploring what it feels like to breathe and what it feels like to sit quietly. Some days, the quiet may bring on the giggles or you may even feel like crying. It is a natural process so don't stress about it or over analyze your reactions, gently guide your mind back to your intention by taking a deep breath.

When you acknowledge that all of these "distractions" are common human nature you may be able to relax more easily. Over time, they are no longer a big deal and you will become more and more comfortable with the quiet.

Lastly, I suggest being kind to self as an intention because often we allow our physical health and awareness to fall behind because we are being more helpful and kind to others than we are to ourselves. A breathing practice is focused time to get to know yourself and be kind to you. Being healthy is the best way to continue to be available to others.

What If I Fall Asleep?

If you do fall asleep during meditation, acknowledge that your body may need more sleep overall. Sometimes if the room is too cozy, warm, or dimly lit your body reads these signs as bedtime signs. It may simply be that you are in need of more sleep in your life or it may be that the environment triggered you to want to sleep.

I used to feel a sense of goodness when one of my yoga students would start snoring. I realized that they felt safe and relaxed enough to doze off. Sometimes our bodies need more rejuvenation than we realize. Our mental and emotional bodies often need rejuvenation more than we acknowledge.

Also, I suggest checking that you are sitting up straight and breathing fully. Slouching while sitting can decrease your energy and oxygen levels and make you less alert.

Setting Intentions

As you continue your breathing practice, having a specific intention for your meditation time will help you determine where you will put your attention. You may decide that you want to focus on more than your breath. Here are some examples of intentions that have to do with the ideas I have mentioned in this book:

- To observe how your breath changes without trying to change its pattern.

- To watch the muscles around your chest or throughout your body relax on every exhale.

- To observe how your body and mind responds to an inhale vs exhale.

- To gently increase the length of the inhale and exhale.

- To internally observe the expansion and contraction of your lungs and diaphragm.

- To note the sensations you feel in your body while meditating.

- To observe the thoughts passing through your mind without getting caught up in any one specific thought.

- To observe how your inhale and exhale change your experience of comfort or discomfort in your body.

- To observe how your thoughts change as the tension or sensations in your body change.

- To be curious how it feels in your body when you are kind to your body and self.

Cues to Follow

I call it a "cue" when I am quietly meditating and I bring something to mind to be aware of or focus on. You will hear me use these during the recorded sessions. Once you have been listening to the recorded sessions and you are practicing on your own, you will begin to say cues in your head as you are sitting quietly. For example, I might say, "Bring your attention to the tip of your nose and feel the air move in and out." The cues should be in line with the intention of your meditation for that day. Cues are also a reminder to focus on what is happening now and can bring your attention back to your breath if it wandered away.

Here Are Some "Cue" Suggestions:

- If your mind has wandered, bring it back to your breath.
- Allow your body to soften (or relax), starting at your head, down your face, releasing your jaw… (and so on as you progress through your body, down to your feet).
- Without changing your breath, see if you can observe its pattern right now.
- Imagine your lungs are like a balloon. When you inhale, allow them to expand in all directions. Up, down, front back and out to all sides.
- Imagine the air entering your lungs is swirling all around, getting into all the creases of your lungs. The air picks up waste and toxins and on the exhale, they are removed.
- Check in with your breath, is it shallow or deep? Can you feel your diaphragm moving?
- Relax your shoulders.

The Logistics of Practicing

- Soften your face, jaw, and tongue.
- Allow your belly to relax and your breath to be easy.
- As you inhale, allow your belly button to expand out and when you exhale, allow your belly button to press back towards your spine.
- Allow your breath to be full yet soft and quiet.
- As you breathe in and out, feel your rib cage expanding and contracting.
- Feel as you breathe in, the slight tension that arises in your chest and how when you exhale that tension releases ... It is subtle.
- As you breathe easily in and out, feel the tension in your body lessen.
- Allow the tension to release from _____ (here you can fill in the blank with a body part.) One day you may focus on the whole body, one part at a time, and one day you may spend the whole time up around the rib cage and dia-phragm.
- Imagine as you increase the depth of your breath, more oxygen is entering your body and being carried through-out your body and up to your brain.
- Bring your attention to an area of injury or pain in your body. On every exhale, imagine tension around that area releasing. As it softens, imagine more blood and oxygen moving in, healing the area.
- Close your eyes, soften your jaw muscles, and allow your teeth to part slightly.

The process of relaxing or softening can feel tedious as you realize how often you have to remind yourself to let go of tension. You may soften and two minutes later that area if tense again. This is all about creating healthy habits.

For instance, once you realize you have extra tension in your shoulders it may take cues in your mind and stretches for weeks before you have the "aha" moment of "Wow, I am actually relaxed in my shoulders." Be patient, decreasing chronic tension in the body takes time and practice.

Review Time

After you settle into a practice and start sitting quietly, you may begin to have insights about your body, mind, spirit, and life in general. For some people, these insights can be marvelous - for some they can be scary. I have had people share that during the breathing practice they were able to breathe better than they had in months. They were astounded by this new-found freedom in their breath and the increase in their awareness. They were very excited. I have also had people share with me that during that quiet time they had memories arise that were emotionally painful and distracting.

Allow a few moments at the end of each meditation for a review of what you may have experienced. If questions or uncertainties arise, I suggest you continue to pay attention to your breath during upcoming meditations. When we sit quietly and breathe day after day, we realize that we don't have to "work it all out" or "rehash" memories for them to resolve. Often, the answers to questions surface and the past dissolves.

For me, I often find that I come up with creative ideas and solutions to personal challenges while paying attention to my breath. I will be completely focused on my breath when "Wham!" a new idea pops so clearly into my mind. I don't have to "figure things out" I just "know." So, if I find myself seeking answers, I now know sitting and breathing is likely the way to find them.

One of the concerns during review time that often comes up for beginners is the question of why they can't easily take a deep breath. Softening is the key. Releasing some of the stored tension in your body will allow you to breathe easier. You are creating a new habit of softening and eventually it will get easier.

Other Ways to Practice Breathing Well

- Integrate breathing practices throughout the day, in small increments, and definitely during your creative endeavors. For example, before starting an activity such as quilting, drawing, writing, driving, reading, making a phone call, etc. do a round of ten full breaths. Or practice breathing fully while doing tasks that you don't need complex thinking such as washing the dishes, mowing the lawn, preparing food for the next meal, organizing your tools, or folding the laundry.

- Watch your stomach moving when you are breathing. (When the stomach moves out, the diaphragm is expanding and air is moving into the lungs. When the stomach moves back towards the spine, the diaphragm is relaxing and air is moving out of the lungs.) Place your hand on your stomach to make that connection in the brain, between breathing and body. This is easier to do while lying down, so if you are about to take a nap, try it then.

- Deep breathing is the calming breath, so it is a useful tool when you feel anxious. Practice deepening your breath and engaging your diaphragm. Practice it during your creative process, when the unknowns arise of what to do next, and observe what happens.

- The bee mantra, in the bonus section, is soothing and calming and the concept, "hum like a bee," is available to anyone. This may also be useful when you have lots of energy and are restless or your mind feels scattered and you want to focus. Making sound is a way to release extra, pent-up energy.

- The rhythm of walking or moving rhythmically may help you focus on your breath more easily. Paying attention to each step or each breath, are two ways you can practice while moving. There is a more about walking meditation in the bonus section.

- Because the mind and the breath are so connected, it can be interesting to practice throughout your activities of the day. Once you are comfortable with the basics and have practiced, you can get more creative and see if there are other ways of incorporating breathing awareness into your day. Sitting meditation is effective but there are many ways to become more intimate with how you are breathing.

Increasing Your Chances of Success

One of the biggest challenges while learning to breathe well is getting past old habits. The way you breathe is a habit and pattern of behavior. Changing it takes the same practice that changing any other habit or behavior takes.

On one hand, you constantly have the opportunity to change the way you breathe since you are breathing in and out several times every minute of the day. On the other hand, it is easy to ignore something you are doing several times every minute of your life. You should treat this like any other attempt to create a new habit. Here are a few suggestions that may help you succeed:

- Set a schedule for when you will sit for a breathing practice. That means scheduling other activities around your commitment when possible. In addition, you might simply set an alarm on your phone throughout the day to remind you to breathe for two minutes.

- Set up a space that has the same chair, aromatherapy warmer, music player, and any other items that you normally use during your meditation time and leave it set up. This way getting settled will take a moment rather than many moments which may give you an excuse to avoid it.

- Set up a time to meditate with someone. Just like any other new habit - friends may help you stick to it. Read this book together and get curious together.

- Talk about it. The more you talk about it, the more it is on your mind triggering you to breathe fully right then and as you talk about it you may be helping someone else learn to breathe well.

- Write about it. Get a journal and write down how you are feeling throughout your meditations. If you are feeling avoidance, fear or discomfort, writing is a great way to work through those feelings. Note changes in how you feel physically and emotionally when you are breathing well. Note when you become aware of new sensations or when you were able to feel the beginning of an emotion before you reacted to it.

Recorded and
Written Sessions

All recorded sessions are at:

www.KellySheets.com/breathe

There are two recorded audio sessions that are the basic meditations of this book. You can download them onto your computer, iPad, or phone, or just listen to them on a computer.

Introduction to Breathing

This recording is a sample of a basic breath awareness.

Decrease Tension

The premise of this session is that the breath is a tool you can use to decrease the tension in your body, ultimately deepening the breath.

On the next page are written versions of these sessions.

Introduction to Breathing:

The intention of this session is to become more aware of your breath. Start in a seated position and allow yourself to get comfortable so that for the next ten minutes you won't be inclined to fidget or move. Place your feet flat on the floor. Scoot your hips back in your chair. Sit up straight, roll your shoulders back, and gently lift your chest. Bring your head back over your shoulders so your ears line up with your shoulders. Let your arms hang down and your hands rest on your lap.

Imagine your spine is getting longer, allowing you to sit up taller. Imagine hips are gently pulling your head towards the sky while your bottom is glued to the chair below you. Once you feel tall and your spine is long, allow yourself to relax as much as possible without beginning to slouch over.

Bring your attention to your breath. Close your mouth and begin breathing in and out through your nose. Become an observer who is watching how your body is breathing.

Soften your jaw, parting your teeth slightly. Allow your tongue to soften, then your throat. Bring your attention to the tip of your nose and begin to feel the small hairs on the inside of your nose moving gently as you breathe in and out. Feel the coolness of your breath as it enters your nose. Allow your breath to be easy, do not try to control the breath, just let your body breathe. Begin to notice the rhythm of your breath. Watch how it changes over time. It is not always consistent. Sometimes you take short shallow breaths, sometimes long, deep breaths; sometimes you pause longer than others between each breath. Watch for a few minutes as your breath changes.

Begin to be aware of your lungs moving while observing your breath. Become aware of the expansion of your lungs as you inhale and their contraction as you exhale. Imagine your lungs are like a balloon with the capacity to expand in all directions. Visualize and feel them expanding side-to-side, front and back, up and down on each inhale. See if you can feel them subtly moving in all directions.

Now focus on the lungs expanding downwards towards your stomach. The muscle at the base of the ribs, the diaphragm, helps the lungs expand down, pulling air in. Then it relaxes, moving back up, pushing the air out of the lungs. Soften your stomach and abdominal muscles. When this muscle expands down you will feel a gentle expansion of your belly. On the inhale, your belly will expand out and on the exhale it will relax back to neutral. If you cannot feel it yet, use your imagination to visualize this movement. This muscle can become stiff from lack of use so visualizing its movement and focusing on the softening of your abdominal area may help you to increase its movement again.

Bring your attention to all these areas of your breath, increasing your awareness of how you are breathing. Move your attention slowly from your diaphragm, your ribs, and your nose. Watch what is happening. While you are breathing, practice increasing the depth of your breath. This should feel like you are allowing your muscles to soften and in turn you will be able to inhale more fully. You should not push or effort to take in more air. Simply continue to focus on softening all the tissue and muscle in your chest area and as that softens you will be able to more easily deepen your breath.

Bring your attention back to the tip of your nose and notice the air moving again. Take a few full, easy breaths. Take one more full breath in through your nose and then out through your mouth. Sit still for another moment and feel the sensations in your body.

Decrease Tension:

The intention of this session is to help you decrease the tension in your body. Start by sitting comfortably in a seated position and allow yourself to get comfortable so that for the next ten minutes you won't be inclined to fidget or move. Place your feet flat on the floor. Scoot your hips back in your chair. Sit up straight and roll your shoulders back to gently lift your chest. Bring your head back over your shoulders so your ears are right above your shoulders. Let your arms hang down and your hands rest on your lap.

Breathe in deeply through your nose and out through your mouth. Do that again and feel what is happening on the exhale. There is a change in the body as you exhale, a feeling of relaxation. Give this some more attention.

Breathe in and out through your nose now, beginning to observe your breath but not trying to control or change it. Observe the expansion and contraction of your lungs. Imagining as they expand front to back, side to side, up and down that you are expanding your rib cage outwards then on the exhale the ribs are slightly contracting back. Allow your body to breathe at its own pace.

Bring your attention to your nose and feel the air move in through your nose, down your throat, and into your lungs - all the way to the base of your lungs. Then watch your breath as it exits the lungs, up your throat, and out through your nose.

Repeat this over and over. Have the simple awareness that you are breathing and that there is a rhythm or quality to your breath. Today, taking a breath might be easy, yesterday might have been more difficult. As you start observing your breath, you start noticing that it changes day-to-day, hour-to-hour. As you become more aware of this, you can use the breath to decrease tension and anxiety in your body.

Begin to notice that as you inhale there is a slight increase in tension in the body and on the exhale there is a slight decrease in tension or a softening. See if you can feel that subtle change. You may want to specifically focus on your chest area or on the base of your throat where it may be easier to feel these subtle changes. For instance, as you inhale, noticing at the base of your throat there is a slight increase in tension.

This practice of noticing these subtle changes is the first step in being able to use this practice on a grosser level. Then you can pay attention through your whole body and relax each muscle. Create an intention that with each exhale you are going to decrease tension in your body. Tension creates tightness around your joints and organs. Tension decreases the flow of blood and fluids that carry oxygen in and waste out. It decreases the ability for healthy blood to get to areas of injury and help healing. It is important to decrease tension and increase fluidity and ease in the body.

Continue to breathe and on each exhale begin to imagine a softening. Check that your jaw and throat are still soft. Bring attention to the areas around your chest cavity, ribs, diaphragm, and back. Allow the tissues in those areas to soften and allow an expansion of your lungs. Notice if there is slightly more movement on the next inhale.

If you don't feel these subtle sensations today, allow the possibility that you will tomorrow or next week. Visualize your body releasing tension as you breathe in and out. Breathing is a practice in subtle awareness and it is just like practicing anything else new.

As you feel the release of tension around your chest area you can begin to move to other areas of your body. Inhale, expanding tissue, exhale, releasing tension. As you decrease tension throughout your whole body you allow for increased overall health.

Bring your attention back to the tip of your nose and notice the air moving again. Take a few full, easy breaths. Take one more full breath in through your nose and then out through your mouth. Then sit still for another moment and feel the sensations in your body.

And Away You Go ...

How to Begin

You are ready to meditate! First, get your space set up with a chair or seat that will be comfortable to sit in.

Sometimes getting started is the hardest part, so here is some direction for the first time you sit to practice:

- Be clear on your intention for the meditation before you start.

- Start by stretching to increase movement and flexibility in your chest area. Do this before every meditation.

- Practice sitting up straight and feeling how that affects your capacity to breathe. Try different ways of sitting up straight with different chairs or pillows to support you.

- Close your eyes and begin breathing in and out through your nose. If your nose is clogged or this is too uncomfortable, begin by breathing through your mouth. Again, you are guiding not pushing. You may be able to start breathing through your nose as you become more relaxed.

- Unless you are doing a walking or moving meditation, remain as still as possible during the meditation. This is a time for internal exploration and being still helps that exploration.

- For the first few times, I suggest doing the meditation titled "Introduction to Breathing" and follow that with "Decreasing Tension" (Both in the previous section)

- End with a brief, quiet review time, allowing yourself to feel what you became aware of. For instance, as you are more aware of sensations in your body, you may notice tingling and warmth in a new area and how it changed when you took a deep breath. Or you may notice how you feel more relaxed or that your breath felt deeper than it did last week. The review allows you to catalog what you are experiencing in your body.

Final Thoughts

Final Thoughts

Becoming more aware of the way you breathe, your thoughts and what you feel in your body is incredibly empowering. In our group program, The Change Militia, we have three tenets which I think are so valuable that I want to share them with you too – be curious, be playful, and be kind.

When I use these in all areas of my life, with myself and others, I grow faster. I become aware of my current limitations and identify areas that I can explore in my life that have historically limited me.

In the past few years, I have grown immensely. I feel more kindness, love, and presence for myself and as a result, others. This is a direct consequence of practices that stemmed from starting a breathing and meditation practice years ago and then developing my sensorial awareness through the practices in The Change Militia. Going within and paying attention to what I am experiencing has truly changed my inside and outside world.

When you start paying attention to your breath, many possibilities open.

Give yourself a chance to succeed by giving yourself time to get comfortable with sitting, meditating, and your own breath. You will find that the more you relax and focus on your breath, the more aware you are of what is going on in your body and how you can change it. If you realize that you can't feel anything or are unaware of yourself, this is a celebration! Because once you realize it, you can practice and start noticing.

And last, as a reminder, enjoy the practice, be playful and have fun!

Choose to be curious, Kelly.

Bonus & Additional Resources

Thank you for reading! I have included two bonus meditation recordings and compiled a list of resources I mentioned in the book. You can find them all here:

www.KellySheets.com/breathe

There are two bonus instructional sessions on the website.

The Bee Mantra

The Bee Mantra is a sound meditation. It is simple and I have found that all ages like this practice. I used to suggest it to my brother when he was stressed because it can be done anywhere, even in the car on the way to and from work. It is great fun because you can change the volume of your bee sound and if you do it with others it can seriously create the buzzing sound of a beehive.

The "buzz" sound you make is actually the NG sound, like in the word running. This keeps the vibrations in your head rather than vibrating out onto your lips, which can feel tickly.

What are the benefits of sound meditation? According to studies shared by Dr. Singh Khalsa in his book "Meditation as Medicine":

- Lowered heart rate.
- Lowered blood pressure.
- Increased feelings of calm and peacefulness due to reduction of stress hormones.

- Removal of toxins (through lymph movement).
- Increased immune function.
- Potential of increased joy due the fun nature of it!!
- Improved memory.

Deep Relaxation

This practice allows you to let go of the stress and tension in your body. Again, doing this at every age is really beneficial to your health. This can be done sitting or lying on the floor or bed. If time is a concern, set a timer or use a recorded meditation so you do not need to worry that you will not get back up. If you are doing this at bedtime, you can relax and fall right to sleep. Close your eyes, go through your body from head to toes or vice versa, soften or release tension, and let it drain out of the body. Then, you allow your mind to relax and stop focusing on anything.

This can last ten to thirty minutes or any length that you feel you need or want.

Increased tension in the body equals increased aging. The body is working all day long. It needs restorative time to release the tension it has held on to. Deep relaxation is a physical, mental, emotional, and spiritual recovery time. In deep relaxation, you allow your body to replenish while the nervous system moves into the relaxation response. It is highly nourishing and regenerative and has a cumulative effect on your entire system.

Notes on Walking Meditation

Walking meditation is the simple practice of walking while paying focused attention to your breath and how you are moving at the same time. The breath can be full and deep when you are doing this practice, so it is another form of breath and sensory awareness. You can do walking meditation in the neighborhood, garden, courtyard, or a long quiet hallway.

The health and flexibility of your feet are vital to your balance. When walking and paying attention, you can become more aware of your feet and how they function, at the same time increasing their health and flexibility.

You can simply choose a space to walk. I like to choose a 15-foot pathway and go back and forth but you can wander on a pathway in any direction. I like to clasp my hands behind my back, stand up tall and begin to walk. With every step you are breathing and simply noticing the placement of your footfalls - heel, arch, ball of foot, now lifting, moving, heel, arch, ball of foot, lifting. Simply note the action of the foot, your attention on breathing, and the movement of your feet. Keep your gaze gently ahead.

The Change Militia

This is our self-paced membership program, which I mentioned has a 100% success rate in helping to alleviate anxiety. It is also where the list of sensations came from. The results of these simple practices range from decreased anxiety, stress, overwhelm, and pain, to better relationships and confident parenting, increased creativity, increased success in business ... the results are pretty amazing. It gives you a simple practice weekly to explore and tools to create more of what you want. No stories, no regurgitation of the past - you start where you are and move forward.

– www.TheChangeMilitia.com

Bali Creatives Retreat

The Creatives Retreat in Bali is an all-inclusive unique opportunity designed to amplify your creativity in an amazing space. The island of Bali is one of the most expressively creative places on earth. If you have an inkling of creative energy flowing, it will amplify it quickly and allow you to express it. If you have a lot of it flowing, it will expand it more and take that potential in new directions. Co-hosted by Kelly and Valori Wells.

– www.BaliCreativesRetreat.com

Kelly Sheets

To learn more about the energizing work that I do to bring the ideas in this book to life for individuals and companies – or if you would like to explore having me speak at your next event, please contact me at:

- www.KellySheets.com, Kelly@KellySheets.com